Irish Arts Center

BOOK DAY
2017

FRIDAY, MARCH 17

Irish Arts Center | NYC

in association with New York City Council, New York State Assembly,
Consulado General de México en Nueva York, Consulate General of Ireland,
Mano a Mano, and Call Me Ishmael

In celebration of outgoing board member James J. Houlihan.

IRISHARTSCENTER.ORG

THEATRE | MUSIC | DANCE | FILM | EXHIBITION | LITERATURE | HUMANITIES
CHILDREN'S EVENTS | EDUCATION | COMEDY | LANGUAGE

#GETLIT at **#IACBOOKDAY**

Gallery Books
Editor: Peter Fallon

SOMEBODY, SOMEWHERE

Alan Gillis

SOMEBODY, SOMEWHERE

Gallery Books

Somebody, Somewhere
is first published
simultaneously in paperback
and in a clothbound edition
on 11 November 2004.

The Gallery Press
Loughcrew
Oldcastle
County Meath
Ireland

ISBN 1 85235 372 4 (*paperback*)
　　 1 85235 373 2 (*clothbound*)

A CIP catalogue record for this book
is available from the British Library.

Contents

for Vincent

The Ulster Way

This is not about burns or hedges.
There will be no gorse. You will not
notice the ceaseless photosynthesis
or the dead tree's thousand fingers,
the trunk's inhumanity writhing with texture,
as you will not be passing into farmland.
Nor will you be set upon by cattle,

ingleberried, haunching, and haunting
with their eyes, their shocking opals,
graving you, hoovering and scooping you,
full of a whatness that sieves you through
the abattoir hillscape, the runnel's slabber
through darkgrass, sweating for the night
that will purple to a love-bitten bruise.

All this is in your head. If you walk
don't walk away, in silence, under the stars'
ice-fires of violence, to the water's darkened strand.
For this is not about horizons, or their curving
limitations. This is not about the rhythm
of a songline. There are other paths to follow.
Everything is about you. Now listen.

12th October, 1994

I enter the Twilight Zone,
    the one run
by Frankie 'Ten Pints' Fraser, and slide the heptagon
    of my twenty
pence piece into its slot. The lights come on.
    Sam the Sham
and the Pharaohs are playing *Wooly Bully*.

A virtual combat zone lights up the green
    of my eyes,
my hand clammy on the joystick, as Johnny 'Book
    Keeper' McFeeter
saunters in and Smokey sings *The Tracks of My Tears*.
    He gives the nod
to Betty behind the bulletproof screen.

Love of my life, he says, and she says,
    ach Johnny,
when who do you know but Terry 'The Blaster' McMaster
    levels in
and B Bumble and the Stingers start playing *Nut Rocker*.
    I shoot down
a sniper and enter a higher level.

Betty buzzes Frankie who has a shifty
    look around,
poking his nut around a big blue door, through which
    I spy
Billy 'Warts' McBreeze drinking tea and tapping his toes
    to Randy
and The Rainbows' version of *Denise*.

On the screen I mutilate a double-agent
　　　　Ninja and collect
a bonus drum of kerosene. *Game of Love* by Wayne
　　　　Fontana pumps
out of the machine, when I have to catch my breath,
　　　　realizing Ricky
'Rottweiler' Rice is on my left

saying watch for the nifty fucker
　　　　with the cross-
bow on the right. Sweat-purls tease my spine, tensed ever
　　　　more rigidly,
when Ricky's joined by Andy 'No Knees' Tweed,
　　　　both of them
whistling merrily to The Crystals' *Then He Kissed Me*.

What the fuck is going on
　　　　here, asks
Victor 'Steel Plate' Hogg, as he slides through the fire
　　　　door. The kid's
on level 3, says Andy. At which point Frankie does his nut,
　　　　especially since
The Cramps are playing *Can Your Pussy Do the Dog*?

Betty puts on Curtis and the Clichés'
　　　　Brush Against Me
Barbarella instead, when the first helicopter shreds the air
　　　　to the left
of the screen. Gathering my wits and artillery, I might eclipse
　　　　the high score
of Markie 'Life Sentence' Prentice, set on October 6th.

I hear Benny 'Vindaloo' McVeigh say,
    right we're going
to do this fucking thing. By now the smoke is so thick
    the screen is almost grey.
The Shangri-Las are playing *Remember* (*Walkin' in the Sand*).
    Frankie says
no, Victor, nobody's going to fucking disband.

Bob B Soxx and the Blue Jeans are playing
    Zip-A-Dee-Doo-Dah.
Through a napalm blur I set the interns free. They wear US
    marine khaki.
Jimmy 'Twelve Inch' Lynch says, son, not bad for 20p.
    I leave the Zone and go
back to the fierce grey day. It looks like snow.

Cold Flow

Presley is singing *In the Ghetto*. The sky is almost blue.
Belfast, under blankets of snow, lies like a letter
not yet written. You aim a cigarette, as though it were a
    snooker cue,
at the red ball of her lips. Which never tasted better.
The hill path is glazed with rippled glass, and you gaze through
a frozen sea of trees, at the town's oyster-bedded pearl,
while smoke fudges the lough like a Cadbury's Twirl™.

While smoke fudges the lough like a Cadbury's Twirl™,
you see colour-fleck cars and butterfly people sprinkling
their hundreds and thousands across the soft icing roads,
    thinking
of singing to Elvis. But she turns away, as if to say how stinking
the snow will become. What a whizz. What a whirl. What a
    girl.
So clever. So bitter. You could have hit her. The sky-dome
    douses
whipped-cream snow, coating the strawberry brick of houses.

Whipped-cream snow coats the strawberry brick of houses,
while aeroplanes levitate like Aero Bars™ over the tip
edge of Belfast's fruit bowl. The sweet snow flies as the
    cloudless
sky cries, and you wipe your runny nose as the cold wind
    blows.
It was the cigarette that tasted good. Not her strawberry lips.
She is melting into the horizon's bones and, as an aeroplane
    drones,
desiccated coconut flakes fall on your face that turns toward
    home.

Desiccated coconut flakes fall on your face, turned toward
    home
laid out like a blanket, through trees that are ice-cream cones.

The melting path sparkles like a Genuine American Miller™ bottle. And 100,000 butterflies will die, jealous of caterpillars, while flowers ignite themselves in protest, then surrender to the infinite cold flow, icing the Milky Way through. Presley is singing *In the Ghetto*. The sky is almost blue.

Street Scene in Blue

The street we once walked paints itself
damson with a lamp lit for shadows,
where figures fade to blue under the lamp's
halo ring, fading into alleyways, into promises
of you. And then my head becomes a DVD
replaying things that were mixed with things
that might have been, intercutting close-ups
with tracking-shots of you next to me,
waiting for friends who arrive in sequence
with a soundtrack, fading from the street scene,
that would give anything for colours no brush can bring.

To Belfast

May your bulletproof knickers drop like rain
and your church-spires attain a higher state of grace.
My lily-of-the-valley, the time is at hand
to ring your bells and uproot your cellulose stem.
I bought hardware, software, and binoculars to trace
your ways of taking the eyes from my head.

And none of it worked. We've been coming to a head
for too long; aircraft prick the veins of your rain-
bow as they shoot you in soft focus to trace
the tramlines of your cellulite skin. But with the grace
of a diva on a crackling screen, you never stem
to their cameras, you're forever getting out of hand.

Once in school, on a greaseproof page, we had to trace
the busts and booms of your body, and I was ashamed to hand
mine in because it lacked what Da called grace.
And I wish I was the centre of a rain-
drop that's falling on your head, the key to your hand-
cuffs, the drug that could re-conjugate your head.

For Belfast, if you'd be a Hollywood film, then I'd be Grace
Kelly on my way to Monaco, to pluck the stem
of a maybell with its rows of empty shells, its head
of one hundred blinded eyes. I would finger your trace
in that other city's face, and bite its free hand
as it fed me, or tried to soothe the stinging of your rain.

Traffic Flow

Letters from Vow and Moneydig are sent to Baltic Avenue,
while from Friendly Row parcels are sent to Drumnakilly
and to Tempo. From Whitehead, past Black Head, and up
to Portmuck, Byron steers his bright red van, dreaming of
Sara in Economy Place, whose handheld has just gone dead.
Down on Cypress Avenue, Katie from Downhill texts Conrad,
lingering in Joy's Entry, listening to *Here Comes the Night*.
She keys 'Sorry but I had 2' while the busker, Sharon, thinks
of phoning home to Gortnagallon. On Dandy Street somebody's
Da says to somebody's Ma: 'Come on to fuck'. It's good to talk.
Moneyglass fills with disillusion. Everybody scampering under
the same weather, crossing lines, never coming together.

Monday Morning

Suddenly I was in the middle of a sex scene
as the green hills huddled like a squad of marines
around the fried-egg sun, in a ketchup-red sky,
which set in relief the coral reef of your eyes.
The six-winged angels programmed an embryo
and the one-eyed wind plucked a terrifying banjo,
while I hobbledehoyed, hoicked my pants off,
took the Obsession on the nose, and thought of
China, the Chinese flag, its picture on TV,
all of this happening to more than me.

Don't You

1

I was working as a waitress in a cocktail bar,
that much is true. But even then I knew I'd find
myself behind the wheel of a large automobile,
or in a beautiful house, asking myself, well,
if sweet dreams are made of these, why don't I travel
the world and the seven seas to Rio, and dance there
in the sand, just like a river twisting through the dusty land?
For though you thought you were my number one,
this girl did not want to have a gun for hire,
no bright spark who was just dancing in the dark.

2

You were working as a waitress in a cocktail bar,
when I met you. And I believed in miracles:
every step you took, I was watching you.
I asked for your name, tipped you again and again
and you said, Don't — don't you want me
to fetch you a drink that would turn your pink mouth blue?
Don't you think this tenth tiny chaser is ten times bigger
     than you?
Don't you talk about places and people you will never know.
Don't you symbolize femininity by use of the letter O.
And I said, Don't you want me, baby? Don't you want me . . .

Windows

At night, by the lamp,
the frame of the window
and the falling stars,
in a constant loop,
rotated on the screen,
like the stars themselves
rotating in the sky.
But the frame of the sparkling graphics
kept dancing.
And I remembered her lithe gymnastics.

❖

The frame of her shoulders,
white as the stars themselves
rotating in the sky,
trampolined into the sky.
She filled the screen
just as the stars of the sparkling graphics
filled up to burst.
I felt their pain — her shoulders doing gymnastics.

❖

Was she repelled by the trampoline
or by the stars themselves
rotating in the sky,
rotating as the darkness
rotates around this lamp,
rotating as her shoulders doing gymnastics
rotated in the gymnasium's light,
bright as the graphics
mimicking her lithe gymnastics?
Or was she repelled by such bright graphics?

❖

Out of the window,
I saw how the moon had circled
like the stars themselves
rotating in the sky.
I saw how the darkness came,
came dancing like the frame of sparkling graphics
and felt alone.
And I remembered her lithe gymnastics.

Love Bites

His slacks slunk to his ankles in a whispering cascade,
revealing 'I love you' on his buttocks' tattooed bouquet.
The tulips he sent her lurched like a fusillade
of fingers that she snipped and tied tightly, her heart's
    tourniquet,
until their bodies gelled together in a thick-set marmalade,
like a bat and ball suspended in a dream-whip ricochet.
But soon his tattoo bled like an overfilled tortilla,
she took a bite but couldn't stop the streaming flotilla
of excuses: the tulips withered, her heart's waterfall
rained down. He drank like Bloody Mary from her castanet
coconut cups of breasts in a last bid to be enthralled,
to embalm the bouquet, on his arse, with this unguent.
Oddly, it worked, and he said 'I'm your snuggleupphagus',
but she was gone. He rammed twelve pints down his
    oesophagus.

Casualty

Car like a comet, breaking all the lights, we speed
towards waiting rooms and vending machines.
The anaesthetic takes time to empty your head
so it becomes a stadium and the game postponed.
Through a window, dead white eyes are staring
upon the sterilized floors, as you lift high
into orbits where the stars have ceased to war:
The Lake Isle of Innisfree, The Forest Moon of Endor.
Then the doctor makes her first incision
with an amphetamine glint in her eye.

Niamh

As sure as fate, in she trickled
    like a long
drink of water, her red head aglow,
    the hieroglyphics
of her obscure face drawing the men's eyes
    through the smoke
as sure as piss-holes through the snow.

'That's why you'll never understand the,
    the immensity of Niamh — '
as broad as I was long, I said 'dead on',
    as if the spiralling
spews of his gabble gobbed me down, my
    rushing host, as if his
spittled chin-wag was a mystic Chiriguano.

I looked back on her, chattering as
    drinks slopped down.
With a draft, the cold still night
    got colder still,
the winds awakened to whirl around leaves
    as I went away
to where duracell disco-tans sweat bombastic

with unbound hair on fantastic
    breasts heaving
to the promise, the smell, of none-can-tell . . .
    'I like the one that goes
Come away' — as she noticed how her magnetic zip
    top drew my burning
eyes, I saw an old mate stick her tongue

through a fella's ear to soothe his brain
        as they played some House
of Pain. Just then, her arms were waving
        as they stretched her
hieroglyphics naked beneath the moon's cool
        beam. I guess her eyes
were agleam as someone gazed on the rush

of blood spurting from her nub of nose,
        and kicked her teeth
to shards, and her stomach. Meanwhile,
        my old mate asks
and 'Yes, I went away,' just like her fella,
        whose head was blown
by talking drums and fizzing forked tongues

leading him astray into the heart of Friday night.
        She said 'fuckim!'
and went away, her flesh presented up from
        her high-heels
en brochette. Along the road to Damascus
        Street, I stopped in
for a curry stain and met Jane

who would later recall meeting Niamh
        stumbling,
stooping for her knickers, flung off outside
        the Vauxhall
with cuts all around her bleeding hair.
        Sirens blare
on the Dublin Road to Damascus, where discarded

diet-Virgin cups bleed into polyester
    slush piles,
as the MultiScreen Palace sweeps
      its Friday diffuse
clean into polyethylene units of ozone
    dust. Tonight's film
was *Eraser* and this town lacks form,

it's like malice through the looking glass
    bombarding past
and presently breaking down. I walk
      on and into
reveries of Niamh, Niamh's propensity
    to call:
Away, come away. Empty your heart.

Last Friday Night

So there wi were like, on the fuckin dance
floor an the skank was fuckin stormin like,
shite-posh, but we'd fuckin chance
it, great big fuckin ditties bouncin, shite,
an thighs, skirts wi fuckin arses man, tight,
that ye'd eat yer fuckin heart out fer. I
was fuckin weltered an Victor was ripe
aff his head cos we'd been round wi Johnny
like, downin the duty-free fuckin gargle, aye.

Anyway, wee Markie must've taken
a few a tha aul disco biscuits like,
loved up da fuck, goin like a mad yin
when some dicklicker came over like, for a fight.
Slabberin! So the fuckin lads go 'right!'
an a huge fuckin mill-up started but
I fucked aff when this tit's head cracked aff a light.
Fuck sake like, my knuckles are still cut.
Shame ye wernie there, ya nut.

Traffic Jam

All along the Lagan was flowing
and the money passed by outstretched hands.
Refugees and a cleavage were blown up on bill-
boards for traffic, which was coming to a head,
when I realized I hadn't turned you on
again. The lipsticked sky smoked contraband
cloud, blurring its tattoo of satellite links,
as I fingered your number into the digital skirl
that threads these streets, full of bodies on the brink
of being found. But your number was dead.

Litter

In one fluent move, I let the crisp bag
fall and licked my salty greased fingers,
then adjusted my balls and watched the empty
packet catch a current, crashing into the kerb,
skipping skyward over fumes of snaking traffic.
Until that evening, fingering peanuts in my dark
blue bowl, with nothing on TV, I never heard
the rustle among the shopping mall's debris,
I never saw the plastics refusing to corrode
among the dockside seaweed, and I lay there,
coiled against the growls of traffic moaning,
the salt-rasped scouring of an outrageous sea.

On a Stark and Boundless Sundown

Where else could I go but away with the fairies
and bums who would dirty my tongue.
Even if you wanted me, I would be contrary
to the map of your eyes. I am a big
girl's blouse, and cannot endure that the streets
could indifferently batter me. The crows
in the wheatfields darken the track overhead,
there is no other. Even the pure dead
brilliant or impure; the healing of one infects another.

There is no interpretation against which to define
myself; I even falter to sign my own condemnation,
due to the trees and the promise of addiction.
Dark nights discard me like the bluster
of north winds, amplifying in their infinite predictions
that lovers will finally bear no resemblance to the stars.
The breath on the glass is the reality of reflection,
the sky's exploded mirror and the birds' radar blips
signify the weightlessness of interiors.

Yet I am part of everything, essential as bacteria
to the microscope. There are many icons
waiting to be clicked, and I am anterior
to anything I might accomplish, though not equal
to the task. I am a permanent desire to be filled in,
like a haulage truck croaking for its diesel.
Sometimes I offer myself, as though a violin,
only to break off before reaching the tune
to end in silence under an immigrant chin.

And if I could I would sing for the colonized moon,
flag-fucked, then abandoned 230,000 miles ago
to circle and glow like a lottery-loser's one glimpse of fortune.

And there is darkness in volume. Influenza music and the
    foreplay
of streets twist into an unripened vineyard of sound,
as lovers writhe with their ears to the ground
and planets recede, to return, at acutely differing speeds:
they want to hear gravity pulling around the orbit
of melodies, the opacity of such foreign tongues.

And it is strange to be on the earth no more,
to quit your yawps and yammers and your promise to run,
every morning, until your lungs have been restored;
strange to not know your name, to be ignored by folklore,
to see patterns that formed immense architectures
churn back to molten vibrations; and being dead leaves me
knackered, in many dimensions, where I hoped for rapture.
Your memories are sounding out the well of yourself
that echoes, and empties, and will not endure.

Dull Weather in Donaghadee

Would to God you could linger by your ships,
letting the days obliterate your conquering lips,
jubilant in their spontaneous gape

teasing time. Your mother had you hung
off her terracotta stairwell: your tongue
trickles out from its pink pale shell

and into the voluptuous mouth of absence.
Corridors. Echoes. The space surrounding you loops
as if its completion were your resemblance,
as fluid as your mother's pea-green soup,

which, I believe, was the object of your mocking
as the photographer took snips
inside, due to bad weather round the rocking
ships. Would to God you could eclipse.

Big Blue Sky and Silent River

Earth a world of stone and woe,
world of stone the earth below;
earth the world of stone echoes,
stone the earth and world also.
Or so you might think as you go
on your rounds through the town, just a stone's throw
from the skirting groves and the hillside's upheaval,
where the river runs through whin burns and hazels.

Cars carousel the hillside's winding hide,
bearing pink pyjamas, white horses, testaments and brides.
A brother picks his nose with his sister's toothbrush;
she rests her feet on his Xbox, the royal flush
of her toenails drying; and on CCTV
a roadsweep is caught catching some zzzs
below the jamboree of pennants, along the alleyways and
    turnpikes,
where everything is lime and gin, terracotta-lite.

Except for you. Eyes to the ground in designer estrangement,
piping-up on skunk with growing agents
in the greenhouse, its higgledy-piggledy tomatoes,
you slabbered on the cobwebbed and gritty Amaretto
that you tea-leafed from a closet at a consolation party,
where no one wanted in your pants and you chundered
    waxed spaghetti,
meatballs, onion, Guinness, and a strangely glowing corncob.
And now, to cap it all, you had to find a job.

You found work in a factory where the engines howled
and your workmates scowled with knuckle-fucked jowls;
where you clocked in, supervised by a clipboard Stalin,
Brylcreem lathering the collar of his sheepskin;
where you became apprenticed to digital power
and dined in a canteen caked in grease and flour;

where the tea was Burmese and the calendars dick-teased,
and you sucked the smoke dreaming of Vladivar and coke.

After you were fired, being considered a safety risk,
you found work in an office where you were barely alive,
tip-tappity-tapping on a flat-packed desk,
obsessed with the efficiency expert's N^o5,
where the files to be sorted with a fine-
toothed sigh ate into your lunch,
into a 'voluntary' overtime
entered into the hard drive's deathless crunch.

And all the boys were drinking and downing,
juiced and trolleyed, swimming and drowning
in Powers and Ladyburn, ouzo and Armagnac,
kvass, aguardiente, Smithwick's and applejack.
And all the town was a halflit-sloshpit-ginbath of a bar
where you got banjaxed and blootered with Brahms and Liszt,
blitzkrieged and bladdered until your eyes became the mist
that blocked the sky and the insatiable stars

which said: the alignment of Venus
suggests today will be a good day
to cast off the past and begin anew.
Seek out that special someone for a rendezvous.
Act kindly if you happen upon a stranger.
Tread carefully, you are in financial danger.
Life at work will reap much satisfaction.
Everywhere may you find some strange attraction.

Around about that time, dilly-dallying home,
she jerked a jug-jiggling move
to her Sony Walkman's remix of a riff by The Edge,
and old Wylie's heart almost leapt out of its bones,
as his tractor somersaulted the shock revelation of groove,

just as your Honda
crashed through the whitethorned hedge,
straight towards harmony and the stars.

Purling bubble, bouncing down the country lane
at summer noon, the glinting river gargling
with springing salmon, bombinating bumblebees,
chirpy birds cheep cheep, and far-off tractor thrum;
bouncing by the trees, to try to tempt her to your bubble,
you saw her fair hair, which simply sent you to the fair,
you kissed that fox-like smirk and teased those nibble-dish ears,
while the auburn fluffy fuzztail of a squirrel chased its nuts.

The glimmer-shimmer-shine of dew droppity dew drops,
dropping off the juicy leaves, left you drinking from
her breast-like nectarines. She had said that she'd be there,
and her hips were threatening to drive you round the bend
to see her smiling, as her ringlets bounced and dazzled
off her sunrise flower neckline, and she spun around
to motion her fruit-gum lips in soft surprise.
And you were paralysed in the marina of her eyes.

So you took her out in your Honda,
with its car-seat covers made of rattle-
skin hide, and drove past the groves to wander
through whin burns and hazels, curbing your tittle-tattle
to study her curlicues, the rhyme of her breath, which
    complimented
the popple and papple of the river's vibrations,
the crow's-feet of her eyes as she squinted
at the cumuli, their thin-veined striations.

Around about that time
you took to drinking with Big Willie Hooks,
who had a bottomless trove of dirty videos and books,

but had lately renounced the hierarchictectitiptitoploftical
　　sublime.
You mostly spent your time chawing on nachos
and Guinness in Mexican-
Irish theme bars, contemplating non-macho
erotica and the enigma of women.

And when you walked with her, you walked into vespers
and dusklight, below the lapwing's ululation
and the indigo sky, losing yourself to the signatures
of the river, its phantom syncopation,
pouring unction and cantatas in the chalice
of her ear; amid viburnum and hawkweed,
you'd roly-poly and clunter and grasp at her knees
in the well-tilled graveyard, its gossamer and malice.

The pepper was in the salt shaker, black in white,
the dark within the light, as you sat at a table for two,
the centre and the satellite. 'It would be great
if it could be kind of loose *and* tight,'
you told her, both actor and playwright.
Then a waiter ended your wait and brought you coffee,
disdain, and desserts to suck and bite,
your latte looking dated beside her latte light.

Big Willie recounted the disaster of being caught in the act.
Stripped to the waist, his upturned arms surrendered, and the
　　Baltic cataracts
trickled right down to his hairless pits, while the surrounding
　　groves
embedded beauty with the precision of the clothes
catalogues in which she'd unleafed herself,
almost down to her forbidden groves of hair.
Behind the master, a comrade pulled off the air,
an image, for Willie, that would forever play with itself.

When she finally made a beeline for your bed,
your numberless nights were almost numbered,
as you tried to enter the crunch of her head
and the sardonyx of her eyes, the amber
of her pelt, her thighs' riverbed,
swinging your huckleboned rumba
on the buttermilk cotton of your bed,
until the morning found you, wildly encumbered.

Around about that time you asked her why all
that diazepam was necessary which she kept under her bed
that slightly jingled and she answered enigmatically, for
   instance,
that the images in your head are an illusion
that imply impressions that limit knowledge
that fails the wits that betray desires
that end in death
that riddles existence.

There were times when you felt you could rip through
the night, that the hug-me-tight
leather of the night
would unzip and pour you
an Absolut vodka and lime,
as you drank in the calamine
and hairspray, the darkshade and tubelight,
your eyes big-widened screens of skybright blue.

She said goodnight sweetheart, it's time to go
where the sky is always blue and you can't hear
the river because the river always flows
in time with the constant atmosphere
that half-forms and tingles the mind and throat,
in measure with the tree shade and the tambourine leaves,

the crow-picker's lustration of the whiskey-tinctured eaves,
and not the flimflam and jissom of these indifferent notes.

You wrote: 'Send me a postcard of everything
I'll never see. Send the Berlin Philharmonic
playing Saint-Saëns *No. 3*. Send me
Poema del cante jondo and the Death of St Valentine.
Send pharmaceuticals, Crave by Calvin Klein.
Nobody here is dancing.
Please send instructions for screwing
someone else's head onto me.'

Big Willie said when God was handing out heads
you must have thought he said beds,
and asked for a big baroque number
with a cool, cast-iron finish.
He produced a bottle of chilled Buckfast wine
and one of his redoubtable Jamaican Woodbines.
You smoked and drank until your eyes were apple-red.
She'll end up in a river, he said.

In your dreams her eyes mellowed into milk
and Kahlua,
and she plunged the queen-size sea of her silk
bed like a dolphin, dancing hula-hulas
until you awakened to a sky of ocean blue,
drinking volcanic water with Tesco's Finest Earl Grey,
as yellowhammers loitered in darkgreen bridleways,
on a screensaver that stayed the night for you.

On other nights you writhed in the dankness of your bed,
a writhing seedbed of termites
that chawed on your eyeballs, on your fetid cheese head,
welting you in the molar crunch of the night,
melting you to corpse juice and meat rot,

death bones and finity and forget-me-nots
igniting you from toe-tip to head,
a red-whipped bushfire of wild-lipped love bites.

Big Willie said the feeling would pass,
as you left him to drive through the grove paths
under an inconstant sky: chameleon grey and greengrey,
carrot, heather, mushroom and ivory,
almond green, lavender, peach-bloom and jasmine,
khaki-flecked, claret, oyster pink and citron,
constantly changing from dove to duck-egg-speckled,
quilted in caramel, biscuit, petrol blue and gunmetal.

You parked to walk by the river, initially in time
with the bubble and rush of its fishscale lather,
but soon you were lost in the bluegrass pantomime
of slurp and bebble and girny-gab glissando,
stopped short by its doo-wop, its pizz-popping jingle-jangle,
its velocious surface of calypso ripple-current
puggling a torrent in a billow-warped refrain,
yammering to rigadoons of light vibronic rain.

You turned away to climb the hillcap,
where the river couldn't reach, through the feverfew
and agrimony, the submarine shit slaps
of snuffle-steaming heifers, where the ash and ember
coloured town, its diminishing corrugations,
fumed below the landfall and vapour trails,
and you looked up where the spoilt sun yoked the sky,
to see if you could see through her cool marine eyes.

You saw a death toll carved in the middle road,
the numbers zip-filed, downloaded holes in the night,
where peace bombs slept behind the schoolyard fence
and cadavers flared their teeth in self-defence;

watched over by satellite,
you took a heavy-booted saunter through demeaning fields
into twilight's velveteen, where the sky became lychee,
the sun's head served on the platter of the sea.

Some day you would wake and find yourself dead
by the river, by the multi-tasking trees,
zephyrs rubbing salt into your hardboiled head
beneath a big blue sky, collapsing to the sea,
the river, river, easing through your bones,
turning to the town, at last, with ghost-drafts
of wisdom, breathing 'Blessed shall they be
who give your children grass instead of stones.'

The choir of the night will intone for her
along the bounds of her impossible river,
where the dead release their vectors
and you anthologize sky-changing eyes
turning to boundless, gazeless blue
through awakening windows in the town
with its turnpikes, its interlocking sectors
under a sun-smirr, coming silently down.

And so you tumbled down the hillside lurching
hither and thither until you finally ran aground,
where you awakened to feel your head without touching
on the outskirts of town, and you found,
beneath the big blue sky, a river flowing into sound
among whin burns and hazels, never to know
what might be benamed and behappened below
the still breathing sky, where the river runs its round.

Deep in the Coral Forest

after Arno Holz

Sea,
sea, sunshiny sea,
as far as you
can see.

Over the bighilly waters,
dinmaking, headtheballing, bellylaughing, carryoncamping,
pleasurebeaching, hurlyburlying, gruntslabbering,
slimslowsliding,
yacketyyacking, yoohooing through the megaphones
of their hands,
seaweedgreenhairy, scaleslipperyskinned, fishtailflippered,
swimdiveglittering, swimrisegleaming, swimsplatspluttering
like mad:
a thousand tritons!

On bright
dolphindorsalfins,
high in a seashell:
a woman!

Oh her ringdingdingalings, her wopbopaloobops,
her lollipoplips, her whollydivine
bucknakedness in the
Sun!

Beneath her drooling, beneath her gabbling, beneath her
dribbling,
constantly approaching
the highwalled, the spangling, the technicolouredthreedimensional
slipperydippery balustrades,
dirty, fat, lecherous
like toads,

seven old, seven slimy,
seven seasplurting,
seabedbristlebearded, seaelephantfartslimy, sealionshockheaded,
walrusquadruplechinbeerbarrelled
seamonsters!

Their ugly mugs!
Their pimplepopped backsnashing!
Their nightmarebreath and disastermovieodours!

Sooner than you could say
hickerydickerydock backwards,
I've leapt superherolike
from behind my
snortneighnosed, hoofthudthumping, arseslapping
bighideglistening, shovelshouldered
twelve-in-hand,
like,
straight into the middle of them!
Zap! Wham! Kapow!
I biffbaff and bitchslap and knuckleknock
their heads.

Oh how they
gurnygobsob
and bawlthewholewayhome!

The lady smiles
and after a beguiling,
charmthepantsoffyou, manoftheworld gesture,
lackadaisically I invite her
with utmost respect
into my bigfish, my kingofthehighway,

my extravagantly
windowsparkling, amberflashing, coralgleaming,
allmodcons twoseater,
then sweep her off into my happydays,
I zoom off
with her into my leatherpaddedcomfy,
I disappear from view
with her
into my delectable, majestical, superduper, topoftherange,
my wonthelotto, most magicalhalflit,
wonderfulunderwater rotatingbedwithmirroredceilinged
purple grotto!

Porter

Draught Guinness becomes the depth of your hair,
outer space within the dead of black: I thought of this
when I pictured the moon of your face, the night
of your locks, as I tipped my tongue into the mercury
head and chilling darkness of my pint, but a television
distracted me as it pronounced an unfathomable score,
and added its reverb or hum to the numinous crack
of the bar's bonhomie, and with so much going on
all around, I almost undervalued the caliginous pint
engulfing the pit of my stomach like a nocturne,
emulsifying my nerves in a silver-lit sea where
I drown in your hair, your raven lie of hair.

Purgatory

Queer thing, there is always music
playing as you skull zombies
and highballs in a hurricane glass,
in the plasma-screened alcove
where she unravelled, at last, to become
a function of your automatic love.
The sky is empty as a keyhole
and the trees are looking in,
and the paintings on the wall
are either fucking blue or fucking green,
as she beckons, wielding a red
hand tattooed on her thigh,
her T-shirt's 'fuck you' with an arrow
pointing up. And you wake into
headwaters coursing, howling onto
your horses, crunching through
your windowpane head, leaving you
on the threshold of discovering
the candour of a melody,
raining to be rendered, undone.

Already dead, as you think them,
your thoughts subside like a riverbed,
swept away with the lime trees and alders,
the fever and the fear, the brochan days
and optic nights coursing everywhere.
Already slipping, your buttery fingers
lose their brakes and take their handles
at the top of the hill, wheels careening
to the dark beneath the hazels, below
the larches and the advertisement sky.
And you always wanted to be Evel
Knievel, and roller-coaster ride
the ocean's upheaval of emeralds
and sapphires, flung on the livid

quilt of a water-mountain's arc.
You wanted to become the blue
and green sides of a creaking open door,
but were forever putting your foot
in your heart as it leapt
from your mouth like a sore.

So they took the words from your mouth
and rented out your home.
They took your speech and wrote 'brains
here' on its back with an arrow
pointing down; and the malignant dial tone
proclaimed there could be no other end,
and the pounding in your head began to cry:
Tonight my eyes turn into television.
Tonight the clouds surrender to the stars.
Tonight the city regrets its subdivisions.
Tonight I drink in non-existent bars.
Tonight the winds are colliding head-on.
Tonight I swim in the aquarium of our bed.
Tonight the whales are singing their depth-songs.
Tonight, my love, you are out of my head.
And now you are always here while she
is always there, in another world you
cannot know, she suspends you over
the current's flow, neither here nor there
but coursing everywhere. And there you go.

You could be going where fields of whiskey
are growing, and the wind moves through her hair.
You could climb to where the half-conscious trees
need nothing but the dereliction of mountains.
You could watch the sun leak into horizons,
the way lily-stems hanker to be oak trees,
the way oak trees lust to be water drops,

dropping like sounds warped together
in a thunder-quilt filling the air,
that could murder for silence; for you could see
the world from here, if it would only stop
curving; you could peel off the label and lift
the lid on yourself, and finally fall
into the hell of your craving, itching in its
scrofulous co-eternity. Or you could stalk
lovers with their tongues unravelling
to a very last kiss, as they miss the draw
and slush of the waves through the night,
vanishing the instant they sight again
the conformingly volcanic dawn.

But now, queer thing, you tread where stalks
uproot the earth with self-profiting intentions.
From dark-hooded hills to harboured coastline,
you lie, and lie for nothing, merely lying there,
the ice cubes of your eyes shot with scarlet,
and all of this lies beyond your comprehension.
But you must ignore the blue and green
combusting as the shoreline suffers
the erosion of the sea, as the sun explodes
the treeshade; you must resist the tempters
saying all this is yours, all you can see,
everything is yours if you be mine.
You must crack yourself, cleave open your nutshell,
where it is never raining, and it is always raining;
where you might be half-dead, or half-alive,
a multiple of zero; where you know nothing
of death zones and birth throes,
these coups and chance meetings of tongues,
their taste, and the teeth in the jar,
or what grows amid the aftershock of rainbows.

Surrender

Surrender the uncountable raindrops
in formation, the migration of birds
by starlight, microbes raving in rock,
a twelve-week strategy for losing self-control,
Guinness is good for you, a riot of
chrysanthemums, surface-to-air consoles,
the infinite non-space of imploded constellations,
the customs officer, the culprit, the illegal distillation,
a symphony of sharks to devour your inner dolphin,
a bar called Galaxy, gigabytes of liberty,
secret doorways to the centre of the mountain.

Waverly and the Rolling Tasman Sea

The roof is still where the puff-scavenged birds will plume
among battalions of headstones, among the tombs.
The sun outlines in repeat freeze-frame violence
the sea, and the sea is perpetually renewed,
like the Chinese student and approaching battletank,
chewed up in the special effects of this silence.

The sun's scoop of honeycomb draws diamonds,
and sapphire horses charge out of the foam.
And the graveyard is a theme-park and its theme
magnificence, a gateway into the tombstones' reticence.
It is here I will drown in the water's secret
hatred and burn in the orange peels of flame.

And I want to be a fruit. Not the fruit
itself, but the fruit dissolved into opulence;
where its taste disappears into a tongue
cell of absence, that's where I'll give myself in
to the violence of the sunset's hurricane.
And this place contains itself, yet explodes

like history with fire. And I like it.
On its head is a glittering marquee made up
of gold, crumbling stone, and half-baked trees.
I hear the cries of large-boned girls,
their grapefruit eyes and icicle teeth lighting up,
like violets and heaven, their heavenly violet lips.

And I will forever dream of that dreaming;
but I cannot tell whether it's benevolence or spite,
both it may be, so deep inside of me.
So none of this will do until I say something
cold as fire and break this diabolic mould
and drink, my lungs, drink up the wind like the sea,

for the wind is rising and away from this place
I must look for the huge air opening and shutting
like a book. And a wave dares to burst and jet
over the peaks, and pages whirl and break
waves, break up rejoicing, break that quiet
roof where the sails peck and scavenge with their beaks.

Aries

One day you might start, poke your crack
and finally dawn on yourself, and climb
out of your sleepy head hollow,
catching a grip to fling wide the peachy
curtains, the stripes on your back
the healing fingers of the blind.

And you might well get up and go,
and tiptoe through this doorway forever,
sashaying through the neverland gardens
by lady's fingers and foxtails, the flushed
tormentils and archangels, tattoos of fritillaries,
Mars burning in the floribunda's glow.

In a nostalgic lapse, you might begin praying
for viral spreads, gnarls, rented alibis
and secret butchers, the avenues and alleyways,
turpentine and zippo, digital eyes preying
on elevator cord-snaps, freak-outs on the motorway,
the fall and phantom lustre of her eyes.

But forget all that, for you will be rolling
with the speedwells and ghost orchids
in your dizzybells and superlation,
the garden spooling into an ever-zooming
city of corundum domes and almandine spires,
the discombobulation of dandillies looming

in souped-up Subarus with their hullaballoo;
and with a rat-a-tat-tat in your temples will you
savour the salt of crizzled skin on your tongue,
the console of your eyes mounting through
the avenues and alleyways, where you will thrive
with shock and awe in the gash of the sun.

Deliverance

Even the trees are on something.
Somebody, somewhere, is almost
making love. Clouds target the hillside,
bringing water, looking for all the world
like spaceships trying to beam themselves down.
Leaves are trapped by the bars of their branches
and aeroplanes guard the blue, as you try
to break through the green prison of your eyes.
Everyone is going to get off.

❖

Unfortunately there are no positions left,
he said. For the record, what can you do?
Somebody, somewhere, is making a killing.
Cigars leer across barstools, asking for a light
now the Sky has been taken from your house.
Then a briefcase tries to sell you up the river.
You shoot the breeze. He talks of a message:
there'd be something in it, all you need do is deliver.

❖

The addicted trees are hooked
on the air. Somebody, somewhere,
is inventing a cure.
Everyone inside is bustling to break out
and the sun has served its time.
Wet dreamers of wide profit margins
drive below the golfball moon,
their speakers selling them life
style options, while you are lying
low. Thieves and lovers gamble in your eyes.

❖

There is a rustling without the windows,
a tinkling in your ear. And somebody,
somewhere, is saved by a machine.
In your dreams you speak to free
heartbeats, dipsticks, ice-floes, smart bombs,
moon men, wolfhounds, death pints,
blue chips, close weather, stem cells, burning discs
and worldwide searches. You speak of bonds.

❖

You wake behind the sun and make
your delivery. There is nothing
in it. The ground beneath your feet
rotates. The planes are on patrol.
Something flies into the pane and dies.
A breeze blows in and everybody profits.
Somebody, somewhere, will understand.
Rub the blue eyes of your windows.
Love is making trees.
You are green under turquoise skies.

Under the Weather

The rain? Don't talk to me about the rain.
A slash of sequins, turning to a drilled
downpour of teeth, gnawing the windowpane,
flushing the roof, gaping the spectrum again.
And we walk the waterbulbs, watching rilled
gutterstreams upsplurge, jetsprouting the drain,
our lagoon-heads pealing into thunder.
Sometime soon, we must talk about the thunder.

Progress

They say that for years Belfast was backwards
and it's great now to see some progress.
So I guess we can look forward to taking boxes
from the earth. I guess that ambulances
will leave the dying back amidst the rubble
to be explosively healed. Given time,
one hundred thousand particles of glass
will create impossible patterns in the air
before coalescing into the clarity
of a window. Through which, a reassembled head
will look out and admire the shy young man
taking his bomb from the building and driving home.

Thou Hast Enlarged Me

I have a filing cabinet of memories
that is not on fire, but incomplete,
as though someone took the files
and scribbled dictations on them.
So I remember things with holes.
I recall eating Hula Hoops — I taste Original
even now, and I know people are attacking
the force. I could be nine, six, or twelve
and three-quarters. Black outlines
on the hill chase after pigs.

Many people are defending the force.
I ask my gym teacher what's going on
and she picks up the phone and asks
'Lord, who shall abide in Thy tabernacle?'
She hangs up looking pleased and tells me,
'Fret not thyself because of evil-doers, neither
be thou envious against the works of iniquity.'
I say thanks Miss and deck Dickie at lunch
because he stole my Original Hula Hoops.
At night I roam the hills and chase piglets.

The hills are above it all; after Trigonometry
I would pass the boarded windows, whose 'No
Surrender' had been defaced with 'No Escape',
and don my robes and chant some Hawkwind,
or daub pentagrams on stone with pigs' blood
Dinger's brother Derek brought up from the abattoir.
Then, one night, they came with hammers and torches
. . . but the file's been tampered with. Over the memory
entitled 'Judge me, O God, and plead my cause
against an ungodly nation', someone has written:

'Dear Al, here's the answers to your questions:
As the heart panteth after water brooks, so panteth my soul
   after thee.
The points of the compass point in opposite directions.
To make a dream come true, keep it secret for three days.
Winter burns, summer melts, autumn soothes, and spring
   begins.
The Middle Irish word for 'province' is *coiced*, literally 'a fifth'.
A thousand years the Earth cried: 'Where art thou?'
Yes, they are currently testing in Antarctica.
The unhappy city always contains a happy city unaware of
   itself.
Tonight — midnight — bring some spirits.'

Killynether

Each time I ignore the stranger in the mirror
on the big wardrobe door, and open wide
its lacquered hatches, lured by the whiff
of dark hanging coats, their Crave and Regal
and their black Quink ink, rubbing my face into
bakeries and florists, the sweat of city buses,

I find another row of jackets where no row could be,
and walk onwards into leather and denim,
limited edition LPs, Lynn or Suzie pouting from empty
Tennant's lager tins, drawing me further into blazers,
football boots and Tupperware lunches,
until eventually, I walk onto Killynether.

At such times I curse my limited imagination.
But then I notice the colour of the grass,
its wet hair hum, and the underworld of tree trunks
and bluebells, the '99' clouds kiss-curling
from Comber to Croob, the peninsula's finger,
and it dawns on me I never knew the names

of ladies' smock or orange tips, the meadow
browns and ringlets; I never walked among
the celandine, silverweed, wood sage and clover;
never listened to the stonechats and linnets,
the stocking creepers fluttering over green-winged
orchids, twayblades, samphire, or elder;

I never caught my shirt on a blazing hedge's
billhooks, by the blackthorn and dogwood,
gliding the breeze with the turnstones and terns,
hawking drumlins and pladdies, following wagtails
and warblers towards Jackdaw Island,
or Darragh Island by Ringhaddy Sound;

I never savoured the wave splash and salt spray,
the sandhoppers feeding on the strandline;
the horse mussels, bulrushes and lugworm casts,
shelducks, oystercatchers, widgeon and snipe
preying on the knotted wrack and eel-grass;
I was never entangled in dense forests of kelp;

I was never dragged beneath the surface
by velvet swimming crabs, to submarine
sand dunes with star pokers and dog cockles
or burrowing brittlestars; I never swam with thornback
rays or nurse hounds to the currents of the Narrows,
coming to rest with anemones and coral.

It's been years since I walked through Killynether.
When I wake I wonder if I've been there ever.
Sometime I must, before I flick the screen
and set about my business, or pick up the telephone,
wander over to the big lacquered wardrobe and open
negotiations with the stranger in the mirror.

When Lying on our Bellies was Brilliant

When one of you burst out of the other
my body butterflied, lightshod hoofbeats
skedaddled from the hubbub for cover,
and we gawped at one another like triplets.
Now the sky's vermilion chills to cool,
and time cuts with brusque abbreviations,
keep in mind when lying on our bellies
was brilliant, when starlings whirled the rose sky.

We opened to all six pearlwort eyes
and jabbled and jibbled through the glades
and wild garlic, as a galaxy of dragonflies
lig-lagged and dizzied the lint-bells and heather
and cool winds absolved the coastline's ablations,
foxtails shushing below the balefires' lilac
where bluehawks birled a spree, hinting the sky,
whose buffets reaved the tummocks
and ripple-grass, always under the weather,
and our arms, stretched wide, reached out forever.

Notes

'On a Stark and Boundless Sundown' is loosely inspired by the first of Rainer Maria Rilke's 'Duino Elegies', and borrows one phrase directly.

'Deep in the Coral Forest' is modelled on, or is a version of, 'Barocke Marine' by Arno Holz.

'Waverly and the Rolling Tasman Sea' is roughly modelled on 'Le Cimetière Marin' by Paul Valéry; its last seven lines are a more or less direct translation.

For their help and encouragement, I would like to thank Ciaran Carson, Peter Fallon, Medbh McGuckian, and my wife, Wendy Townsend. The completion of this book was greatly facilitated by my employment at The Seamus Heaney Centre for Poetry at Queen's University, Belfast, and I would like to thank all those associated with it.